the GodMan

infinite love **encapsulated** in a finite moment

by Stanley Kenji Inouye

Published by Iwa, Inc.
P.O. Box 3796
Gardena, CA 90247-7496

First Edition

Cover Art
Yoshihiro Ishida

Cover Design and Layout
Stanley Kenji Inouye

ISBN 978-0-9835238-1-9

the God Man

DEDICATION

This poem is dedicated to my parents, Ariaki and Ida Inouye, and to my wife, Janie, and daughters, Heather and Joelle.

Without their steadfast love and support throughout the years, *The GodMan* poem would have never reached completion.

It is my hope and prayer
that the blessing that they have been to me
will bear fruit in the lives of many others.

SKI

INTRODUCTION

JAPANESE CALLIGRAPHY

The Japanese calligraphy on the **front cover and to the left** is an artistic representation brushed by Yoshihiro Ishida of the Japanese character, *kami*, meaning god. The more complex character, *kami*, is a combination of two simpler characters meaning "to show," and "to speak." In other words, the Japanese word for god, *kami*, implies that **God is a "show and tell" God**, that he reveals himself through both words and concrete actions.

This is consistent with how God is described in the opening verses of the historical account of Jesus' adult life written by John—one of his closest followers. These verses read as follows:

> **In the beginning the Word already existed.** *The Word was with God, and the Word was God. He existed in the beginning with God. God created everything through him, and nothing was created except through him. The Word gave life to everything that was created, and his life brought light to everyone. The light shines in the darkness, and the darkness can never extinguish it.*
>
> **So the Word became human and made his home among us.** *He was full of unfailing love and faithfulness. And we have seen his glory, the glory of the Father's one and only Son.*
>
> John 1:1-5,14 NLT

In these verses, Jesus is referred to as the "Word." As such, Jesus existed before the world began. He created everything and gave life to all that lives. Very directly, this passage tells us that Jesus was not only with God when all these things occurred, but was, in fact, God himself. Finally, these verses reveal that this same Creator and Life Giver became a human being and entered human history, that person being Jesus. So then, **Jesus is both God and Man.** That is why this poem is entitled *The GodMan*. It is about Jesus. It looks at the entire Bible as the story of how Jesus relates to all he created—past, present and future. This poem speaks not only of the beauty and perfection of Creation's beginning, but also of its tragic and gradual demise. Then unfolds what Jesus, the Creator, has done and will do so Creation will ultimately become more wondrous and glorious than ever—forever!

The purpose of *The GodMan* poem is to introduce the reader to the Person the Bible refers to as the "visible likeness of the invisible God." By becoming acquainted with the concrete and finite Jesus of history, the reader can come to understand and identify with the invisible and infinite God of eternity. More amazing still, it becomes eminently clear through Jesus' perfect personification of God that this very same invisible and infinite God wants to have an interpersonal, day-to-day relationship with each of us, and did what was necessary so that such a relationship is now possible.

METAMORPHOSIS

Stanley Kenji Inouye wrote *The GodMan* poem shortly after his daughter, Joelle, passed away from Spinal Muscular Atrophy at the age of 16. Writing the poem helped Stan to find the hope and assurance he needed as he **grieved** over Joelle's death. After *The GodMan* was written, **Yoshihiro Ishida meditated** upon one page of the poem each week as a way of centering his thoughts and prayers. As an image would come to mind while meditating, Yoshi **pencil-sketched** the image that he envisioned. He then **photographed** various objects and scenes in and around his home to provide himself with a digital palette from which to choose color, shape and texture so they could be **combined** to recreate the images imprinted upon his mind while meditating.

AUTHOR

Stanley Kenji Inouye ("Stan") graduated from the University of California, Berkeley with a degree in Landscape Architecture. Ever since then, he has been involved in full-time Christian ministry. Stan has held national and international responsibilities with Campus Crusade for Christ and has taught classes and seminars periodically at Fuller Theological Seminary. He has also published articles included in a number of Christian books and magazines. He was the first national director of Asian American Christian Fellowship, a ministry of Japanese Evangelical Missionary Society. He has spoken widely at retreats and conferences throughout the United States, and served as a consultant to churches, denominations and parachurch organizations. In 1981, Stan founded the ministry of Iwa, which seeks to assist Christians and churches to more effectively relate the essential meaning of the Bible to Asian Americans, especially Japanese Americans. Stan is married to his beautiful wife, Janie, and has two incredibly creative daughters, Heather, and Joelle who now lives on with the Lord in heaven.

ARTIST

Yoshihiro Ishida ("Yoshi") is a graduate of the prestigious Art Center College of Design. He is an award-winning auto designer and Japanese calligrapher, presently pursuing a career in fine arts. His grandfather, who was a Japanese carpenter, greatly influenced Yoshi's sense of aesthetics and appreciation for the close relationship between spirit and nature. Yoshi is a committed Christian who passionately desires every aspect of his life to reflect the transformation he is experiencing as a result of having the Spirit of Jesus at work in and through him, including his art. Yoshi is married to his wonderful wife, Barbie. Yoshi is a gourmet Japanese cook and is also an expert at restoring antique Japanese art and furniture.

ACKNOWLEDGEMENTS

The GodMan poem is a miracle! It could not have been produced without the expertise, talent, perseverance and prayers of a host of passionately committed volunteers. It all started when **Derek Kamemoto**, then an Iwa Board member and now an Iwa Advisory Board member, reviewed a different presentation of the essential message of the Bible that Iwa was working on; he called it "poetic prose" and suggested that Iwa choose between poetry or prose. After its completion, **Yoshihiro Ishida** voluntarily prayed and meditated on each page of The GodMan poem—mostly on Sundays for over a year—staying with each page until God provided him with a representational image of its contents.

All along the way, Iwa staff, both past and present, have offered their help and support with the editing, formatting, producing and distributing of The GodMan poem. They include **Cyril Nishimoto, Ellen Fukuyama, Danny Matsuda, Dorothy Kirkland** and Stan's daughter, **Heather Inouye.** Iwa's Board of Directors and supporters have also been essential in providing the time, space and funding necessary so that the Iwa staff and volunteers could do what was necessary for The GodMan poem to be completed.

And, Stan is additionally deeply grateful to family and friends who have been a constant source of prayer, encouragement and help throughout the entire twelve years it took to finally produce and distribute The GodMan poem, especially his loving and patient wife, **Janie.**

AVAILABLE VERSIONS
Gallery
Once the images for each of the 37 pages of The GodMan poem were completed, they were **custom formatted** into what we refer to as the Gallery Version. This version of the poem was designed for **limited distribution** due to its high cost and labor-intensive production. This form of its presentation was recommended by internationally known painter and arts advocate, **Makoto Fujimura**, who suggested the poem and visual art be formatted and presented in precisely the way that the images were conceived. Each page of the poem would be laid out by itself on a blank sheet of paper. The corresponding image to each page of the poem would then follow on its own exclusive page. These pages would be unbound so that the reader/viewer could move from page to page in the same way as the visual images were created by Yoshi. Later, it was decided that each page of the poem would be printed on obscure translucent vellum so that the corresponding image would show through, hinting at the relationship between each page of the poem and its parallel visual expression.

The quality of the vellum and paper together with its presentation box and handmade interior were meticulously chosen and designed because what is presented is the most precious message in all eternity. The poem and its related abstract art seek to communicate the most essential meaning of the Bible. Life and death literally weigh in the balance for everyone who ponders it. For those who embrace its message, this precious box holds "Good News"—the assurance of an eternal, loving and living relationship with God starting right now!

The entire boxed presentation of the Gallery Version of The GodMan poem is acid-free and archive-safe. Rather than just another book to be read once and then stored, forgotten and gathering dust on a bookshelf somewhere, this version of The GodMan has been designed to be enjoyed and shared over and over again for a lifetime and more.

Paperback

A paperback version which includes **both the art and text** of *The GodMan* poem is also available. The words and art are bound side-by-side on left and right matching pages.

Text Only

The **format in hand** is the Text Only Version of *The GodMan* poem. This version has been published for **wide distribution** at an **affordable price**.

FUTURE DEVELOPMENT

In the future, either the **Paperback** or **Text Only** Version may also be **used as reference** when listening to or viewing electronic media of the poem, visiting a gallery exhibit or attending a live performance of *The GodMan* poem. Please check our website at **www.iwarock.org** for information about the development and availability of new versions and formats.

the poem begins...

Realize it or not . . .

God loves us
        beyond comprehension
        beyond imagination
        boundless

more than the unquenchable passion of first love
more than the heartache of a mother missing her child
                lost
                kidnapped
                      or suddenly dead

Experience this love
        the source of all love
           through the love story
           without which
                there would be no love stories

God invites us,
    "Enter my heart . . .
        Let me tell my story . . . "

    It starts . . .
        where love begins
           before Creation . . .

              before land or sea
                plant or beast

              before you or me

Before time . . .

God existed . . .
three were One
One was three
God the Father
God the Son
God the Spirit

They formed
a home
a family
a bond of shared intimacy
unshakeable
unbreakable . . .
heaven defined

In each other
they took delight
they gave to each other
all each possessed
no one possessed any one thing
but all possessed everything
freely
generously
fully
they gifted each other
totally of themselves

This is love

the center of God's heart

Out of that center
        everything was created

As still alpine lakes mirror sky and mountain
        all there was
                reflected the Three
                        who are One
                                yet three at once
                each piece of Creation's glory
                        uniquely different
                                yet mysteriously the same
                        bore a mark
                                of common origin . . .

                                        the mind of God

        The Three who are One
                declared
                        all things "good"
                                including us
                        both male and female
                                two from one
                                two who could become one again
                        each uniquely different
                                yet mysteriously the same
                more than anything else
                        we too bore a mark of common origin . . .

                                        the heart of God

We shared God's home
                and belonged to God's family
        we delighted in each other
                shared all we possessed
                        lost ourselves in one another
                savored life
                        seasoned with laughter
                cherished love

                aware of God's ever-presence
                        secure
                        safe beyond measure
                        at peace
                                in harmony with the universe

But we were not love's prisoners
        choice exists where love abides
                Freedom is love's watchword
        God freely chose us
                now we were free to choose
                    or
                not to choose
                    God

Tragedy struck
        we chose ourselves—
                doubting God's goodness
                    believing God to be a deceiver
        we trusted only in ourselves
                to make God's design reality
                        that we would be like God
            which
                ironically
                    we already were
                        but now no longer

with no sky or mountain to reflect
        still alpine lakes are ice cold emptiness
so we became . . .
        ice cold emptiness
                beyond God's warmth
                devoid of God
                    as counselor
                    as comforter
                    as constant companion
                        as spiritual life source . . .

We now gazed into self-made mirrors
                to discover only dark shadows
                faint silhouettes
                    of the brilliant reflections of God
                we once were

Mankind's downfall dragged the universe in its wake
        spiraling downward
                toward ultimate destruction and despair

                falling dominoes
                        tumbling faster and faster
                                the momentum mounting
                                in direct proportion to the terror
                                our inevitable demise imparts
                        to the deepest recesses of our souls
                                where denial is our only defense

We shun the threat that daily knocks
        on our tightly locked but flimsy doors . . .
                burglary
                rape
                murder
                war
                        flagrant symbols
                                of everyday violations
                                        which victimize us all

Alcohol and drugs
        television
        computer games
        the Internet
                cars
                clothes
                bigger and bigger houses
                                man-made religion—
                        self-medications
                        all

                        anesthetizing us
                                numbing our sensitivities
                                        our sensibilities
                                to the reality
                                our misguided arrogance
                                        led us—

                        believing we could be god-like
                                without God having the right
                                to be God
                                        in our lives

17

Our godless overindulgences
                    have choked
                            clogged
                                    contaminated
                    earth, river, sea and sky
                                    making all species
                    endangered without exception

            The final demise—
                    relational dysfunction
                            families shattered
                                    persons isolated
                                            by
                                            dislocation
                                            distrust
                                            disloyalty
                                            dismay
                                            despair
                    worse yet
                            the spiritual family
                    flip side of the human family
                            our relationship with
                                    God the Father
                                    God the Son
                                    God the Spirit
                    the Many who are One
                            as we were designed
                                    and destined to be
            also shattered beyond recognition
                    dysfunction
                    a diminished description—
                            harvest of our fatal error

        not only our relationship with God ripped apart
                but God's heart
                    torn
                    grief struck
                            by our betrayal

    How could we
            Creation's pinnacle
                    the "spittin' image" of our Creator
            Creation's greatest ecstasy
                    dare become
                            Creation's only disappointment
                            Creation's only disgrace
                            Creation's only destroyer?

                            How dare we?

We did dare
and
through the life God gave
death was sown

We
once God's dream
now God's nightmare
became God's obsession

love and indignation battled
mercy prevailed
love became the victor
pushed God the Father

to do
the unpredictable
the unprecedented
the unparalleled

He sent his Son
to save and salvage
the broken pieces of his Creation
including us
especially us
the very ones who broke Creation
broke ourselves
broke God's heart
the heart of Father
the heart of the Son
the heart of the Spirit

all Three

God the Son
      entered human history
            a baby

        miraculously born to a young unwed virgin

              Mary

        adopted by her fiancé
           a Jewish carpenter

            Joseph

        born in a stable
           roughly two thousand years ago
               in Roman-occupied Israel

        named
             Jesus

        meaning "God the Savior"

Jesus
>God the Son
>>son of God the Father
>son of Joseph
>>his human father

>totally God
>>totally human

>called both
>>Son of God
>>Son of Man

>>grew up
>>matured
>>>mentally
>>>emotionally
>>>spiritually

>>before emerging
>>>Son of God

>>>in a rough-hewn
>>>>human body
>>>skilled at a trade
>>>>with no formal education
>>>without wealth

This same Jesus
    healed
        a leper
            by a simple touch of his hand
        a blind man and a deaf mute
            with his saliva
        a woman bleeding internally
            with the mere edge of his clothing
                glancing the tip of her finger
        a paralytic
            with a word of forgiveness

This same Jesus
    brought the dead to life again

        A true story—
    a close friend lay dying
        the sister begs him to come
            he waits two days
                arrives too late
            he weeps
                but then commands,
                    "Come out!"
                his friend emerges from the tomb
                    alive again

        Another true story—
    a Jewish religious leader
        his daughter deathly ill
        pleads,
            "Please come . . ."
    Jesus follows

        delayed by the healing of another
            the daughter dies

        amidst the wailing
            Jesus deems it sleep
                not death
            the mourners laugh
                but then
        Jesus tells her to awake
            she rises
        walking among them

This same Jesus
    cast out evil spirits
        near and far
            by the authority of his command

This same Jesus
        manipulated matter . . .

                        He
                multiplied matter . . .
                        fed thousands of hungry people with a few fish
                                and a couple of loaves of bread
                transformed matter . . .
                        turned water into wine
                                at a wedding feast
                transcended matter . . .
                        walked to a boatload of his disciples
                                on turbulent seas
                        commanded a raging storm to stop
                                        it
                                stopped

                        He
                dematerialized matter . . .
                        passed through locked doors
                                                after his death
                        miraculously appearing
                                amidst a huddle
                                of his fearful followers
                                        who
                                        not only saw
                                but touched
                                        then
                                        at last
                                        truly
                                        believed

                matter didn't matter
                        to Jesus

Jesus did the expected
             if
             you are
             Son of God
                        come to earth

                             healing
                                        exorcising
                             water to wine
                                        multiplying fish
                             walking on water
                                        calming storms
                             materializing and dematerializing

         but
         far more

Jesus did the unexpected
               more amazing still
                   he was
                             so human
                             truly human
                                        the way we-were-supposed-to-be
                                                         human
                             He
                             Son of God
                                        took care of his mom
                                                  loved kids
                                        told stories
                                                  and jokes
                                        romped
                                        wrestled
                                                  and hugged—
                                                         his unwritten policy
                                                  kids always welcome

                             He
                   hung out with outcasts
               poor and pitiful
         preferred the promiscuous
         over the pompous and powerful
                   touched untouchables
                        forgave the unforgivable
                                  favored the irreligious

                                  loved everyone
                             including his accusers
                                        and abusers

Jesus was human

more human than we are
too human to be human

yet he was human
and
God
both

not half God and half human

not God sometimes
and
human other times

but

human as we were
designed to be

God at one with us
we at one with him
always
and forever

Jesus did miracles
not by the power and authority
of being God's Son

but
with divine rights surrendered

he did what he did
as a human
with no supernatural abilities

totally trusting God the Father

doing everything
for him
depending upon him
in partnership
with him
by God's power
working through him

Jesus was more human
than we who are human

because
he was
as we were

before we betrayed
Father
Son
Spirit

trying to be like God
on our own
rather than human
with God's help

Irony of ironies
when we are truly human
we are truly god-like

for that is what God
purposed for us

to be
his reflection
his image

god-like
but never God

Jesus showed us
God the Father
packaged in human flesh

also
showed us
us

us
as we were meant to be
human flesh
surrendered to God
a package for
God's character
God's power
God's love
a reflection of the Father
as we were
in the beginning

But
      what did we do
         to the
         Son of Man
         perfect reflection of God
         Jesus

         also

     Son of God
         "visible image
             of the invisible God"
         the reflection's perfect source?

         After he
befriended us
healed us
purged us of our demons

fed us
taught us
affirmed and corrected us

       we
       turned on him

sneering
       jeering
judging
       persecuting
mocking
       torturing
hanging him on a cross

       destroying his body

The cross
        the crucifix
                a symbol
                multifaceted

symbol of what we did to God
symbol of what we did to Man

                we shattered
                both

                        Source
                        and Reflection

we broke God's heart
we broke God's image

but Jesus' body was not symbolically broken
                history attests
        his body was
                in fact
                        stretched and torn
                        limb from limb
                                hanging
                                pinioned
                                        feet and hands
                                        to a wooden cross
                                pierced with a spear
                        tip of stone cold steel
        shocking warm flesh
hot from the torment of strained muscles
                        taut but gradually giving way
        tired of trying to keep itself
                from becoming its own assassin
                suffocated by its own weight
        lungs crushed by a collapsed ribcage
                beneath skin and tissue
                pulled to their limits

Why?
The beginning
      so innocent
      so pure
      so good
The outcome
      so treacherous
      so wrong
      so horrifically bad
Why?

    At first
Jesus pleased everyone
      built up our hopes and expectations
we praised him
      treated him as new king

but then
      we couldn't control him
        he disillusioned us
          disappointed us

what could have been
      his grand coronation
        became
        to the crowd
          a farce
      Jesus entered the holy city
          hailed by joyous multitudes
        riding on a donkey
          Instead of a stallion
        ridiculous
we
the masses
      mesmerized by him still
      would have followed him
          anywhere
he could have usurped power
      freeing many
        of malicious
          greedy
          oppressive
          rulers
      but no
he taught, "Love your enemies . . .
      do good to those who persecute you"

      he embarrassed us

Our old religious leaders
        deceitful
           self-serving
               manipulative
     but
   at least
     not weak
        cowardly
        sissies

        like Jesus

   Jesus wasn't guilty of anything
       apart from
          loving
          and
          forgiving

        his only flaw
             perfection

     but
        jealous of him
        convicted by his goodness
        hating him
        believing him
          a heretic
   the leaders seized opportunity
        to turn our frustration
               into
               rationalization
        for his execution

       Opportunity knocked
            the leaders turned the knob
        we
        the fickle crowd
          rushed
          through the door

       The outcome
     the Son of God
       Son of Man
         put
         to
         death

But it didn't have to be that way
        on that cross
                Jesus didn't have to stay

    after all

                he was Son of God
                    who
                            made the blind to see
                                the lame walk
                                the storm stop
                he was Creator

    A mocker mocked,
            "If you are Son of God,
                come down . . ."

        he could have
                whenever he wanted
                        but he didn't
            he chose to suffer and die

                    Why?

God the Father
God the Spirit
        could have stopped the torment
                        stopped the torture
                            stopped the death
                                but
                                didn't

                    Why?

31

"Oh, God!"
what torment was his
what torture
what death

as Spirit and Father
stood by
enduring their own crushing agony
as the Son was whipped
crowned with thorns
puncturing his anguished brow
forced to shoulder
his own cross
amid taunting throngs
once filled with adulation
for Jesus
their long hoped for

Savior

Through crowded city streets
the Son of God
Son of Man
dragged that foul instrument of execution
to the hill
called "Skull"

There the sound of hammer on nails
resounded
pounded
through wrists and feet
into wood
onto stake and beam
of that hideous cross

now heavy
with the weight of
Jesus' body stripped naked

The cross

now scraping
along dirt and pebbles
on its way to the hole
dug deep
to provide secure anchorage
for the top heavy
body-laden pole—

mast for the cross

The cross slides
        then sinks
                crashing
                        into the dark pit
        a loud hollow sound resounds
                momentum and gravity
        pulling body mass downward
                past the stopping point
                        of flesh imbedded nails

        ripping
                tearing not only skin and sinew
                but
                heart and soul

    not only of Jesus
        the Son
                but of Father
                        and Spirit also

                God
                ripped apart

                        God forsaken
                        by God
                                himself

                        Son separated
                        from Father

                        Father separated
                        from Spirit

                a first
                and last
                        in all eternity

Seconds trickle by
        pooling into minutes

        then hours

                a seeming eternity
                                encapsulated
        in a portion of one day

                                infinite agony
                                        in a finite moment

33

As sun passes overhead
    his body
        like a carcass impaled on a stick
            waiting for vultures to pick its bones
                bakes beneath the arid sky
       moisture depletes
            imperceptibly at first
      then
            unmistakably
      finally
            parched beyond endurance
      a gnawing yearning erupts
                Jesus cries out,
                    "I thirst!"

But nothing offered
      will ever quench his greatest thirst
the thirst of soul and spirit
      as Father and Spirit both
        refuse
            holy communion and comfort
                the oneness and assurance
                before
                always present
            now withdrawn
                painfully withheld
causing excruciating agony for all alike
            Father
            Son
            Spirit

          Creation responds to
              the Creator's anguish

              pitch black darkness
              envelops everything

              everywhere

              Creation's sun refuses light
                as life's light
                fades
                within
                the
                Creator's Son

Jesus' suffering

                    crescendos
            his cries grow louder
                    increasingly
                    incessantly
                    louder within
        from whisper to scream
                    but never reaching his lips

            at last
            the end comes

        what little life remains
                    bursts forth
                        audible

    "My God, my God, why have you forsaken me?"

        "It is finished!"

"Father, into your hands I commit my spirit"

                    then
                    the heaving
                    stops

                    eerily

                        dead silence
                        follows

            saturating the darkness

Suddenly
the ground beneath
        first rumbles
        then shakes
        finally rattling
                clattering
                roaring
                        like an anguished
                        angry
                        lioness
                crouching
                over the limp body
                of her dead cub
                        slain
                        by a predator
                        who dared kill
                        the predator's
                        own prince

        rocks and boulders
                        split
                tombs open
                        the dead walk
                        among the living

fear grips

        terror sets in

            panic finds voice

                    feet take flight

To insure death
 a spear finds its way
 to the center of Jesus' body
  core of his being
 puncturing
 what was
 emotionally
 spiritually
 punctured already

 All remaining
  body fluids
  gush forth

  spattering
  the earth below
   a crimson stain
   enlarging
   by every throb
   and fraction
   of each second

bled
 from the Creator's
 own corpse
  a blatant blotch
  signifying
   Creation's
   ever-growing
   shame

Why

this seemingly senseless bloodshed?

 What gives reason for such sacrifice?

 No intellectual abstract reason will suffice

 Only the logic of love

Jesus didn't have to die
            but he did

he died voluntarily
        by choice

            suicide?
                    surely not
                    not to escape
                    not out of cowardice
                            or self-inflicted guilt
                            shortcoming
                            failure

the death he died
        we deserved
                    for the brokenness we caused—
                        Creation
                        ourselves
                        most of all
                                God

                                        Father
                                        Spirit
                                        Son

        we
        who should have brought
                    our Creator
                ultimate
                honor and glory
        brought
                uttermost
                shame

God created beauty and order

        we created distortion and chaos

38

Jesus died
    a martyr's death
        uncompromising
        unbending
        unwavering
        unselfish

    for truth
    truth worth dying

    what truth?

        God loves us
        no matter what

            loves us still

            no matter how we
                abuse him
                accuse him
                refuse him

      he will
            pay any cost
            make any sacrifice
            suffer any pain

      to prove
            beyond doubt's shadow

            God loves us

Jesus died
            a hero's death
              like a
              brave soldier
              rushing back
                    amid gunfire
                          mines
                          and missile blasts
                to save
                      not only
                            his fallen friends
                but also
                      how absurd
                      his fallen foes

      Jesus died
            a lover's death
              like Romeo
              like Juliet
                    if death ushers in sweet reunion
                    then
                    death's horror
                          is wantonly embraced
                          endured
                                to gain
                                eternal oneness

Jesus' death

    the cross
    a billboard
    for all to see

    a giant exclamation point
    ending
    God's plea

        of Father
        of Son
        of Spirit
            all Three

    begging us,
        "Can't you see . . .

    "Can't you see
        what you have done
            to me
                Father
                Son
                Spirit
                    the Source
                    all Three!

        And to
        you too
            the Source's Reflection

    bleeding
    broken
        beyond all description

        due all
            to your
            ill-conceived
                ill-gotten
                    illusion of emancipation
                      free from me
                      but slave to self . . .

. . . Please! I beg you. Come back to me!"

So
what is our answer
to God's desperate plea
reflected through Jesus' suffering
for all to see?

The cross
but a brief peek
a passing glimpse
into God's heart

a glance
at the pain
endured
ever since
our rough
ragged start

when first we refused
to put trust in his love
and pursued
our own dreams
instead of
his design
from above

all because
we wanted
to be
our own gods
instead of
God's own

how sad
but now
how glad

all we must do
is say "yes" to the cross
and God will forgive
and embrace us
not counting his loss

What loss?

the loss of his Son

But wait
the story doesn't end there
Jesus didn't stay dead

taken down from the cross
his body buried
entombed in a cave
sealed shut
by
an enormous stone
entrance blocked
a Roman seal
bearing the governor's likeness
death awaiting any
who dare
break it
and open the tomb

Roman soldiers
around the clock
standing guard
insurance
no one will . . .
open the tomb

No one could
no one did
but
during the night
early morning
the third day

something
miraculous
happened

cataclysmic

fright struck
soldiers fled
leaving the tomb
abandoned

wide open

Women
        timid yet courageous
            came to mourn

                the site empty
                        desolate
                        deserted

                soldiers
                        gone

                stone
                        rolled away

                cave
                        wide open

                corpse
                        missing

        but not empty
                after all
        light radiates
                from the darkness
                        of the tomb

        frightened
                curious
                the women
                        cautious
                        enter

        ablaze in white
                and bright light
                an angel
                        greets them
                announcing
                        Jesus
                        Son of God
                        Son of Man
                        dead
                        now
                        risen
                        not dead
                        not missing

                            but alive again

walking
talking
hugging
eating

appearing
as he once was
but not really

physical
but also
metaphysical

materializing
dematerializing

passing through
          solid matter
vanishing

he appears
          first
                    to a few
          then
                    to many
          finally
                    to a multitude

                    for days
                    for weeks

                    before
                    ascending

                    up

                    higher

                    higher

                    higher

as eyes follow

          until
                    clouds

                    become his shroud

disappearing

      returning to his Father
          God the Father

    so that
          he
          God the Son
          could send

          his Spirit
          God the Spirit

    to us
    who believe

    to indwell
        to fill
        to overflow

empowering
those who say "yes" to the cross
      sorry for God's pain
      sorry for God's loss

        to change
        be transformed

          so
          bit by bit
            little by little
          person by person
            life by life
          group by group
            family by family
          culture by culture

    endangered species by endangered species

        the pieces
        of our
          broken lives
          broken homes
          broken cultures
          broken world

      can be fixed
          put back together
            cracks eliminated
            the face of Creation
              wiped crystal clear

to reflect
once again
as all should
the creativity and character
of our Creator

God the Father
God the Son
God the Spirit

all three

in oneness and unity

bringing glory to God

not shame
upon his name
or
disgrace
upon his face

but

delight

joy

laughter

pleasure

to God

to others

to ourselves

to all living things

in peace and harmony with the universe

forevermore!

So
what about you
        your life
        your relationships
                with
                God
                others
                and
                the whole of Creation?

Are you part of Creation's restoration
                or
                complicit
                in its further
                        continued
                        ultimate
                                annihilation?

Are you
        healing God's wound
        or
        making it worse

                growing deeper

                ever more painful?

What will you do?

        The choice is up to you

                Freedom is love's watchword
                        gift from a loving God

                        Nothing
                in all Creation
                        could bring God

                                more satisfaction

                        more fulfillment

                                more honor

                        more joy

                than if we choose
                        to respond to his love

        by receiving his love

and

loving him back

The choice is yours

and yours alone

only you can choose

What will you do?

Back Cover Symbol

The logo in the center of the back cover is not only a symbol representing the Christian organization that published *The GodMan* poem. More importantly, it represents Jesus as the Son of God.

The name of the organization is Iwa which is a Japanese word describing a huge boulder or high stone cliff that cannot be moved or manipulated by human beings. At the same time, it is molded and shaped by the natural elements surrounding it. The currents of wind, rain and water impact its appearance without ever changing its fundamental nature. *Iwa* aptly describes Jesus as the infinite and eternal God who allowed himself to become a finite and historical human being so that we might be able to know who he is and how deeply he wants to have a loving, interpersonal relationship with us. It is no wonder that *iwa* is used in the Japanese Bible to refer to the Lord as the Rock of Our Salvation.

The logo is a symbolic representation of an enormous natural rock or stone monolith being buffeted by ocean waves symbolized by a traditional Japanese wave pattern.

Iwa

P.O. Box 3796
Gardena, CA 90247-7496
(626)398-3468
email: iwarock@aol.com
www.iwarock.org

To obtain information about Iwa, *The GodMan* Bible study series, or the many resources offered by Iwa, to order additional copies or versions of *The GodMan* poem, or to donate to Iwa, please go to www.iwarock.org or contact Iwa.

www.ingramcontent.com/pod-product-compliance
Lightning Source LLC
Chambersburg PA
CBHW060541030426
42337CB00021B/4377